© EMMA DODGE HANSON

FRANK BIDART

STAR DUST

Frank Bidart's most recent full-length collections of poetry are *Desire* (FSG, 1997) and *In the Western Night: Collected Poems 1965–90* (FSG, 1990). He has won many prizes, including the Wallace Stevens Award, and *Star Dust* was a National Book Award finalist. He teaches at Wellesley College.

ALSO BY FRANK BIDART

GOLDEN STATE

THE BOOK OF THE BODY

THE SACRIFICE

IN THE WESTERN NIGHT: COLLECTED POEMS 1965–90

DESIRE

AS EDITOR

THE COLLECTED POEMS OF ROBERT LOWELL
  (*ed. with David Gewanter*)

STAR DUST

STAR DUST

FRANK
BIDART

Farrar, Straus and Giroux
New York

Farrar, Straus and Giroux
19 Union Square West, New York 10003

Distributed in Canada by Douglas & McIntyre Ltd.
Printed in the United States of America
Published in 2005 by Farrar, Straus and Giroux
First paperback edition, 2006

Some of these poems first appeared in The Atlantic Monthly, Bloom, Daedalus, Harvard
Magazine, The Literary Review, The New Yorker, Ploughshares, Poetry *("The Third
Hour of the Night"),* Raritan, Salmagundi, Slate, The Threepenny Review, Tin House,
and TriQuarterly.

Music Like Dirt *was published as a chapbook by Sarabande Books in 2002.*

*"An Interview with Frank Bidart," by Adam Travis, is reprinted with the kind permission
of Bookslut.com.*

The Library of Congress has cataloged the hardcover edition as follows:
Bidart, Frank, 1939–
    Star dust / Frank Bidart.—1st ed.
      p. cm.
    ISBN-13: 978-0-374-26973-9
    ISBN-10: 0-374-26973-4 (alk. paper)
    I. Title.

PS3552.I33S73 2005
811'.54—dc22

                2004056293

Paperback ISBN-13: 978-0-374-53033-4
Paperback ISBN-10: 0-374-53033-5

www.fsgbooks.com

10 9 8 7 6 5 4 3 2 1

CONTENTS

I

MUSIC LIKE DIRT

Bound, hungry to pluck again from the thousand
technologies of ecstasy

boundlessness, the world that at a drop of water
rises without boundaries,

I push the PLAY button: —

. . . Callas, Laurel & Hardy, Szigeti

you are alive again, —

the slow movement of K.218
once again no longer

bland, merely pretty, nearly
banal, as it is

in all but Szigeti's hands

·

Therefore you and I and Mozart
must thank the Twentieth Century, for

it made you pattern, form
whose infinite

repeatability within matter
defies matter—

*Malibran. Henry Irving. The young
Joachim.* They are lost, a mountain of

newspaper clippings, become words
not their own words. The art of the performer.

MUSIC LIKE DIRT

FOR DESMOND DEKKER

I will not I will not I said but as my body turned in the solitary
bed it said But he loves me which broke my will.

music like dirt

That you did but willed and continued to will refusal you
confirmed seventeen years later saying I was not wrong.

music like dirt

When you said I was not wrong with gravity and weird
sweetness I felt not anger not woe but weird calm sweetness.

music like dirt

I like sentences like He especially dug doing it in
houses being built or at the steering wheel.

music like dirt

I will not I will not I said but as my body turned in the solitary
bed it said But he loves me which broke my will.

That man's own life is an object for him. That animals
build nests, build dwellings,

whereas man contemplates himself

in the world that he has created:
That you cannot find yourself in your labor

because it does not belong to your essential being:

That estranged from labor the laborer is
self-estranged, alien to himself:

That your nature is to labor:

That feeling himself fleetingly unbound only when
eating, drinking, procreating, in his dwelling and dressing-up,

man erects means into sole and ultimate ends:

That where he makes what he makes, he is
not: That when he makes, he is not:

Thus the ground of our self-estrangement.

—Marx in 1844, before the solutions that he proposed
betrayed him by entering history, before, like
Jesus, too many sins were committed in his name.

FOR BILL NESTRICK (1940–96)

Out of the rectitude and narrow care of those who
teach in the public schools,—

                                a mother
who would not let her son watch cartoons of
Porky Pig because we must
not laugh at someone who stutters,—

. . . the mystery, your brilliant
appetite for the moment.

        •

For Herbert, the aesthetic desideratum is

*unpremeditated art, not as "natural" or "spontaneous"
but a speaking of the Spirit as it becomes
conscious, a fidelity to*

the moment itself. The only

*appropriate gift is discovered to be
inseparable from
the giver, for man can only give himself.*

In 1975, the magazine that printed your great essay
announced: *He is writing a book on Herbert.*

        •

You lived in the realm where coin of the realm
is a book,

and despite the fact that by the end of
graduate school you
already had published twenty thousand articles

you never published a book.

Against the background of this bitter
mysterious lapse your brilliant
appetite for the moment.

LITTLE FUGUE

at birth you were handed a ticket

beneath every journey the ticket to this
journey in one direction

or say the body

is a conveyor belt, moving in one direction
slower or swifter than sight

at birth

you were handed a ticket, indecipherable
rectangle forgotten in your pocket

or say you stand upon a moving walkway

as if all you fear
is losing your

balance moving in one direction

beneath every journey the ticket to this
journey in one direction

There is something missing in our definition, vision, of a human being: the need to make.

•

We are creatures who need to make.

•

Because existence is willy-nilly thrust into our hands, our fate is to make something—if nothing else, the shape cut by the arc of our lives.

•

My parents saw corrosively the arc of their lives.

•

Making is the mirror in which we see ourselves.

•

But *being* is making: not only large things, a family, a book, a business: but the shape we give this afternoon, a conversation between two friends, a meal.

•

Or mis-shape.

·

Without clarity about what we make, and the choices that under-
lie it, the need to make is a curse, a misfortune.

·

The culture in which we live honors specific kinds of making (shap-
ing or mis-shaping a business, a family) but does not understand
how central making itself is as manifestation and mirror of the self,
fundamental as eating or sleeping.

·

In the images with which our culture incessantly teaches us, the
cessation of labor is the beginning of pleasure; the goal of work is
to cease working, an endless paradise of unending diversion.

·

In the United States at the end of the twentieth century, the great-
est luxury is to live a life in which the work that one does to earn a
living, and what one has the appetite to make, coincide—by a kind
of grace are the same, one.

·

Without clarity, a curse, a misfortune.

·

My intuition about what is of course unprovable comes, I'm sure, from observing, absorbing as a child the lives of my parents: the dilemmas, contradictions, chaos as they lived out their own often unacknowledged, barely examined desires to make.

•

They saw corrosively the shape cut by the arc of their lives.

•

My parents never made something commensurate to their will to make, which I take to be, in varying degrees, the general human condition—as it is my own.

•

Making is the mirror in which we see ourselves.

•

Without clarity, a curse, a misfortune.

•

Horrible the fate of the advice-giver in our culture: to repeat oneself in a thousand contexts until death, or irrelevance.

•

I abjure advice-giver.

Go make you ready.

STANZAS ENDING WITH THE SAME TWO WORDS

At first I felt shame because I had entered
through the door marked *Your Death*.

Not a valuable word written
unsteeped in your death.

You are the ruin whose arm encircles the young woman
at the posthumous bar, before your death.

The grass is still hungry
above you, fed by your death.

Kill whatever killed your father, your life
turning to me again said before your death.

Hard to grow old still hungry.
You were still hungry at your death.

THE POEM IS A VEIL

V E I L,—as if silk that you in fury must thrust repeatedly
high at what the eye, your eye, naked cannot see

catches, clinging to its physiognomy.

LUGGAGE

You wear your body as if without
illusions. You speak of former lovers with some

contempt for their interest in sex.
Wisdom of the spirit, you

imply, lies in condescension and poise.

. . . Fucking, I can feel
the valve opening, the flood is too much.

Or too little. I am
insatiable, famished by repetition.

Now all you see is that I am luggage

that smiles as it is moved from here
to there. *We could have had ecstasies.*

In your stray moments, as now in
mine, may what *was not*

rise like grief before you.

HAMMER

The stone arm raising a stone hammer
dreams it can descend upon itself.

When the quest is indecipherable, —
. . . what is left is a career.

What once was apprehended in passion
survives as opinion.

To be both author of
this statue, and the statue itself.

INJUNCTION

As if the names we use to name the uses of buildings
x-ray our souls, war without end:

Palace. Prison. Temple. School.
Market. Theater. Brothel. Bank.

War without end. Because to name is to possess
the dreams of strangers, the temple

is offended by, demands the abolition of brothel, now theater, now
school; the school despises temple, palace, market, bank; the bank by

refusing to name depositors welcomes all, though in rage prisoners each
night gnaw to dust another stone piling under the palace.

War without end. Therefore time past time:

Rip through the fabric. Nail it. Not
to the wall. Rip through

the wall. Outside

time. Nail it.

HEART BEAT

ear early tuned to hear beneath the call to end
eating flesh, sentient suffering beings (creatures

bred now for slaughter will
then never be bred)   *less life*   *less life*   tuned to hear

still the vow solemn and implacable I made as a kid
walking a sidewalk in Bakersfield

never to have a child, condemn a creature
to this hell   as the prisoner

chorus in wonder is released into the sun, ear early tuned to hear
beneath the melody the ground-bass   *less life*   *less life*

LEGACY

When to the desert, the dirt,
comes water

comes money

to get off the shitdirt
land and move to the city

whence you

direct the work of those who now
work the land you still own

My grandparents left home for the American

desert to escape
poverty, or the family who said *You are the son who shall*

become a priest

After Spain became
Franco's, at last

rich enough

to return you
refused to return

The West you made

was never unstoried, never
artless

Excrement of the sky our rage inherits

there was no gift
outright   we were never the land's

LAMENT FOR THE MAKERS

Not bird not badger not beaver not bee

Many creatures must
make, but only one must seek

within itself what to make

My father's ring was a B with a dart
through it, in diamonds against polished black stone.

I have it. What parents leave you
is their lives.

Until my mother died she struggled to make
a house that she did not loathe; paintings; poems; me.

Many creatures must

make, but only one must seek
within itself what to make

Not bird not badger not beaver not bee

.

Teach me, masters who by making were
remade, your art.

II

CURSE

May breath for a dead moment cease as jerking your

head upward you hear as if in slow motion floor

collapse evenly upon floor as one hundred and ten

floors descend upon you.

May what you have made descend upon you.
May the listening ears of your victims   their eyes   their

breath

enter you, and eat like acid
the bubble of rectitude that allowed you breath.

May their breath now, in eternity, be your breath.

       •

Now, as you wished, you cannot for us
not be. May this be your single profit.

Of your rectitude at last disenthralled, you
seek the dead. Each time you enter them

they spit you out. The dead find you are not food.

Out of the great secret of morals, *the imagination to enter the skin of another,* what I have made is a curse.

KNOT

After, no ferocity of will could the hand

•

uncurl. One day, she joked, I'll cut it off.

•

OPEN. Her hand replies that flesh insulted by being cannot bear to

•

wake. OPEN. She repeats the word to what once was hers

•

but now not.

PHENOMENOLOGY OF THE PRICK

You say, Let's get naked. It's 1962; the world
is changing, or has changed, or is about to change;
we want to get naked. Seven or eight old friends

want to see certain bodies that for years we've
guessed at, imagined. For me, not
certain bodies: one. Yours. You know that.

We get naked. The room
is dark; shadows against the windows'
light night sky; then you approach your wife. You light

a cigarette, allowing me to see what is forbidden to see.
You make sure I see it hard.
You make sure I see it hard

only once. *A year earlier, through the high partition between cafeteria
booths, invisible I hear you say you can get Frank's
car keys tonight. Frank, you laugh, will do anything I want.*

You seemed satisfied. This night, as they say,
completed something. After five years of my
obsession with you, without seeming to will it you

managed to let me see it hard. Were you
giving me a gift. Did you want fixed in my brain
what I will not ever possess. Were you giving me

a gift that cannot be possessed. You make sure
I see how hard
your wife makes it. You light a cigarette.

On the surface of the earth
despite all effort I continued
the life I had led in its depths.

So when you said cuckoo
hello and my heart
leapt up imagine my surprise.

From its depths some mouth
drawn by your refusals of love
fastened on them and fattened.

It's 2004; now the creature
born from our union in 1983
attains maturity.

He guards the frontier.
As he guards the frontier he listens
all day to the records of Edith Piaf.

Heroic risk, Piaf sings. Love
is heroic risk, for what you are impelled
to risk but do not

kills you; as does, of course this voice
knows, risk. He is addicted
to the records of Edith Piaf.

He lives on the aroma, the intoxications
of what he has been spared.
He is grateful, he says, not to exist.

ROMAIN CLEROU

When I asked if she was in pain he said
No but that she had in her final minutes showed that panic

he had often seen the faces of the dying show facing the void.

He said this matter-of-factly, as if because he was
a doctor his experience mattered, as if he had known

her and her son long enough not to varnish or lie.

They had gone to high school together and now
because he had become a doctor and then become

her doctor he watched Martha face the void.

Twenty-eight years later, I can hear the way he said
Martha. His name was Clerou: Dr. Romain Clerou.

HADRIAN'S DEATHBED

Flutter-animal
talkative
unthing

soon from all tongue unhoused

where
next

forgotten
voiceless
scared?

SONG

You know that it is there, lair
where the bear ceases
for a time even to exist.

Crawl in. You have at last killed
enough and eaten enough to be fat
enough to cease for a time to exist.

Crawl in. It takes talent to live at night, and scorning
others you had that talent, but now you sniff
the season when you must cease to exist.

Crawl in. Whatever for good or ill
grows within you needs
you for a time to cease to exist.

It is not raining inside
tonight. You know that it is there. Crawl in.

STAR DUST

Above the dazzling city lies starless
night. Ruthless, you are pleased the price of one

is the other. That night

dense with date palms, crazy with the breath-
less aromas of fresh-cut earth,

black sky thronging with light so thick the fixed

unbruised stars bewildered
sight, I wanted you dazzled, wanted you drunk.

As we lie on our backs in close dark parallel furrows newly

dug, staring up at the consuming sky, light
falling does not stop at flesh: each thing hidden, buried

between us now burns and surrounds us,

visible, like breath in freezing air. *What you ignore or refuse
or cannot bear. What I hide that I ask, but*

ask. The shimmering improvisations designed to save us

fire melts to law. *I touched the hem of your garment. You opened
your side, feeding me briefly just enough to show me why I ask.*

Melancholy, as if shorn, you cover as ever each glowing pyre

with dirt. In this light is our grave. Obdurate, you say: *We
are darkness. We are the city*

whose brightness blots the stars from night.

THE THIRD HOUR OF THE NIGHT

When the eye

When the edgeless screen receiving
light from the edgeless universe

When the eye first

When the edgeless screen facing
outward as if hypnotized by the edgeless universe

When the eye first saw that it

Hungry for more light
resistlessly began to fold back upon itself   TWIST

As if a dog sniffing

Ignorant of origins
familiar with hunger

As if a dog sniffing a dead dog

Before nervous like itself but now
weird inert cold nerveless

Twisting in panic had abruptly sniffed itself

When the eye
first saw that it must die   When the eye first

Brooding on our origins you
ask *When* and I say

Then

                    •

wound-dresser   let us call the creature

driven again and again to dress with fresh
bandages and a pail of disinfectant
suppurations that cannot
heal for the wound that confers existence is mortal

wound-dresser

what wound is dressed   the wound of being

                    •

Understand that it can drink till it is
sick, but cannot drink till it is satisfied.

It alone knows you. It does not wish you well.

Understand that when your mother, in her only
pregnancy, gave birth to twins

painfully stitched into the flesh, the bone of one child

was the impossible-to-remove cloak that confers
invisibility. The cloak that maimed it gave it power.

Painfully stitched into the flesh, the bone of the other child

was the impossible-to-remove cloak that confers
visibility. The cloak that maimed it gave it power.

Envying the other, of course each twin

tried to punish and become the other.
Understand that when the beast within you

succeeds again in paralyzing into unending

incompletion whatever you again had the temerity to
try to make

its triumph is made sweeter by confirmation of its

rectitude. It knows that it alone
knows you. It alone remembers your mother's

mother's grasping immigrant bewildered

stroke-filled slide-to-the-grave
you wiped from your adolescent American feet.

Your hick purer-than-thou overreaching veiling

mediocrity. Understand that you can delude others but
not what you more and more

now call the beast within you. Understand

the cloak that maimed each gave each power.
Understand that there is a beast within you

that can drink till it is

sick, but cannot drink till it is satisfied. Understand
that it will use the conventions of the visible world

to turn your tongue to stone. It alone

knows you. It does
not wish you well. *These are instructions for the wrangler.*

II

Three Fates. One
fate, with three faces.

Clotho   Lachesis   Atropos

Thread spun by one
from all those forever unspun.

Thread touched by one and in
touching twisted into something

forever unlike all others spun.

Thread touched by one and in
touching withered to nothing.

Atropos   Lachesis   Clotho

Three, who gave us in recompense
for death

the first alphabet, to engrave in stone
what is most evanescent,

the mind. *According to Hesiod, daughters of Night.*

•

"Unless teeth devour it it
rots: now is its season.

My teeth have sunk into firm-skinned
pears so succulent time stopped.

When my wife, dead now

ten years, pulls her dress over her petticoats
and hair, the air crackles, her hair rising

tangles in ecstasy. We are electric ghosts.

•

You hear the strange cricket in the oven
sing, and ask what it sings.

This is what it sings.

Because *Benvenuto* in my native tongue
means *welcome*, write

here lies an artist who did not
recoil from residence on earth—but,
truly named, welcomed it.

But I mis-spoke: not *wife*. Servant: model: mother
of my child, also now dead.

                    •

In prison, immured in the black pit where the Pope
once fed Benedetto da Foiano less and less each day
until God's will, not the Pope's own hand, killed him,—

where outside my door each day the castellan
repeated that darkness will teach me I am
a counterfeit bat, and he a real one,—

blackness, silence so unremitted
I knew I had survived another day only by the malignant
welcome singsong of his triumphant voice,—

Benvenuto is a counterfeit bat, and I a real one,—

where God had not found me worthy of seeing the sun
even in a dream, I asked the God of Nature
what unexpiated act the suffocation of my senses, such

suffering, served to expiate.

(This was my first prison.)

•

For the two murders I had committed,—their just,
free but necessary cause

revenge, however imperfect the justice—

two successive Popes recognized the necessity
and pardoned me. *Absolved* me.

Because my fame as a maker in gold and silver

preceded me, though I was hardly more
than an apprentice, when Pope Clement came into

possession of the second largest diamond in the world

he summoned me from Florence to Rome—called me
into his presence to serve him. To crown the resplendent

glittering vestment covering his surplice, he wanted

a golden clasp big and round as a small
plate, with God the Father in half-relief above the diamond

and cherubs, arms raised, below. *Hurry*, he said,

finish it quickly, so that I may enjoy its
use a little while.

Pope Clement, unlike the great I now serve, was

an excellent, subtle
connoisseur; he approved my design.

Each week he summoned me into the presence

two or three times, eager to inspect my progress.
Then Cecchino, my brother, two years younger than I

and still beardless, died—

was killed, as he tried to avenge the unjust killing of
a comrade by the ruthless guard of the Bargello.

Thus was stolen from him the chance to incise

his presence into the hard, careless surface of the world.
The fool who killed him

in what justice must call self-defense

later proved his nature by
boasting of it.

His boasting enraged, maddened me. In this

great grief the Pope rebuked me: *You act as if*
grief can change death.

Sleepless, eatless, by day I worked at the Pope's

absorbing golden button—and by night, hypnotized
as a jealous lover, I watched and followed

the fatuous creature who murdered my brother.

At last, overcoming my repugnance to an enterprise
not-quite-praiseworthy, I decided

to end my torment. My dagger entered the juncture

of the nape-bone and the neck
so deep into the bone

with all my strength I could not pull it out.

I ran to the palace of Duke Alessandro—for those who
pursued me knew me. The Pope's natural son,

later he became Duke of Florence, before his murder

by his own cousin Lorenzino, whose too-familiar
intimacies and pretensions to power

he not only indulged but openly mocked.

Alessandro told me to stay indoors
for eight days. For eight days I stayed indoors, working

at the jewel the Pope had set his heart on.

For eight days the Pope failed
to summon me. Then his chamberlain, saying that all was

well if I minded my work and kept silent, ushered me

into the presence. The Pope cast so menacing
a glance toward me I trembled.

Examining my work, his countenance cleared,

saying that I had accomplished a vast amount
in a short time. Then he said, *Now that you are*

cured, Benvenuto—change your life.

I promised that I would. Soon after this, I opened
a fine shop, my first; and finished the jewel.

                    •

As the knife descended (forgive me, O God of
Nature, but *thus* you have arranged it,—)

to my fevered mind
each moment was infinite, and mine.

                    •

Late one night, in farewell, Michelangelo
turning to me said, *Benvenuto,*

you deliver yourself into their hands.

•

Here I leapt   Here I leapt   Here I leapt   Here I leapt
the shrilling cricket in the shrilling summer evening

sings; as did my father in the sweet years

he served the pleasure of the lords of Florence
as a piper, in the Consort of Pipers.

Imagine my father, no longer young, married, still

childless, an engineer who designs bridges and
battlements for the Duke, but whose

first love is music — the flute. He joined

the Duke's Consort of Pipers. Now his nights
often are spent not bending over charts and plans

but dazzled at the court of Lorenzo, called *The Magnificent* —

the same Lorenzo who once plucked Michelangelo, still
a boy, from among the horde of the merely-talented

bending to copy the masters in the ducal palace.

Lorenzo, with his father's consent, adopted
the boy; fed him at his own table.

Imagine, tonight, the brief concert is over—

the Consort of Pipers (respectable, honorable
amateurs: small merchants, a banker, a scholar)

mingle, slightly awed, with an ambassador, a Cardinal . . .

Suddenly Lorenzo is at my father's ear: *He stood
not six inches from me.*

Not six inches from my father's ear Lorenzo

in a low voice as he begins to move through
the crowd followed by his son Piero

(as now my father must struggle to follow)

tells my father he has painfully and increasingly
remarked that the flute has led my father to neglect

his fine engineering talent and therefore my

father will understand why Piero and the Duke
must dismiss him from the Consort of Pipers.

Lorenzo, entering the private apartments, was gone.

In later years, my father repeated to his
children: *He stood not six inches from me.*

It is a lie. It is a lie that the Medici and you and I

stand on the same earth. What the sane eye
saw, was a lie: —

two things alone cross the illimitable distance

between the great and the rest of
us, who serve them: —

a knife; and art.

      •

The emblem of Florence is the lion; therefore
lions, caged but restless and living, centuries ago

began to announce to the Piazza della Signoria

this is the fearsome seat of the free
government of the Republic of Florence.

Duke Cosimo, hating the noise and smell, had them

moved behind the palace. For years, I had known
the old man who fed and tended the lions, —

one day he humbly asked me if I could make a ring

unlike all others for his daughter's wedding.
I said yes, of course; but, as payment for its

rarity, I wanted him to drug the strongest lion

asleep, so that I could
examine, for my art, his body.

He said he knew no art of drugging; such poison

could kill the creature; a week later,
in fury he said yes.

The animal was numbed but not

sleeping; he tried to raise
his great head, as I lay lengthwise against his warm body;

the head fell back. My head

nestling behind his, each arm, outstretched, slowly
descending along each leg, at last with both hands I

pulled back the fur and touched a claw.

This creature whose claw waking could kill me,—
. . . I wore its skin.

•

After the Medici were returned from eighteen years'
banishment, placed over us again not by the will

of Florentines, but by a Spanish army—

my father, though during the republic he regained
his position as piper, ever loyal to the Medici

wrote a poem celebrating his party's victory

and prophesying the imminent
advent of a Medici pope. Then Julius II died;

Cardinal de' Medici, against expectation, was elected;

the new pope wrote my father that he must
come to Rome and serve him.

My father had no will to travel. Then Jacopo

Salviati, in power because married to a Medici,
took from my father his place at the Duke's new court;

took from him his profit, his hope, his will.

Thus began that slow extinguishment
of hope, the self's obsequies for the self

at which effacement I felt not only a helpless

witness, but
cause, author.

He said I was his heart.

I had asked to be his heart
before I knew what I was asking.

Against his mania to make me a musician

at fifteen I put myself to the goldsmith's trade;
without money

or position, he now could not oppose this.

Help the boy—for his father is poor
rang in my ears as I began to sell

the first trinkets I had made. Later, to escape

the plague then raging, he made me
quickly leave Florence; when I returned,

he, my sister, her husband and child, were dead.

These events, many occurring before my birth, I
see because my father described them

often and with outrage.

To be a child is to see things and not
know them; then you know them.

                    •

Despite the malicious
stars, decisive at my birth: despite their

sufficient instrument, *the hand within me that moves*

against me: in the utter darkness of my first prison
God granted me vision:

surrounded by my stinks, an Angel, his beauty

austere, not wanton, graciously
showed me a room in half-light crowded with the dead:

postures blunted as if all promise of change

was lost, the dead
walked up and down and back and forth:

as if the promise of change

fleeing had stolen the light.
Then, on the wall, there was a square of light.

Careless of blindness I turned my eyes

to the full sun. I did not care
to look on anything again but this. The sun

withering and quickening without distinction

then bulged out: the boss
expanded: the calm body of the dead Christ

formed itself from the same

substance as the sun. Still on the cross,
he was the same substance as the sun.

·

The bait the Duke laid
was Perseus. Perseus

standing before the Piazza della Signoria.

My statue's audience and theater, Michelangelo's
David; Donatello's

Judith With the Head of Holofernes . . .

Here the school of Florence, swaggering, says
to the world: *Eat.*

Only Bandinelli's odious *Hercules and Cacus*

reminds one that when one walks
streets on earth one steps in shit.

Duke Cosimo desired, he said, a statue of Perseus

triumphant, after intricate trials able
at last to raise high

Medusa's mutilated head—he imagined,

perhaps, decapitation of the fickle
rabble of republican Florence . . .

I conceived the hero's gesture as more generous:—

*Kill the thing that looked
upon makes us stone.*

Soon enough, on my great bronze bust of the great

Duke, I placed—staring out from his chest—
Medusa, her head not yet cut, living.

                    •

Remember, Benvenuto, you cannot bring your
great gifts to light by your strength alone

You show your greatness only through

the opportunities we give you
Hold your tongue   I will drown you in gold

                    •

As we stared down at the vast square, at
David, at *Judith*—then at *Hercules and Cacus*

approved and placed there by Cosimo himself—

from high on the fortress lookout of the palace,
against whose severe façade so many

human promises had been so cunningly

or indifferently crushed, I told the Duke that I
cannot make his statue. My brief return from France

was designed only to provide for the future of

my sister and six nieces, now without husband
or father. The King of France alone had saved me

from the Pope's dungeon — not any lord of Italy!

At this, the Duke looked at me
sharply, but said nothing.

All Rome knew that though I had disproved

the theft that was pretext for my arrest, Pope Paul
still kept me imprisoned, out of spite —

vengeance of his malignant son Pier Luigi, now

assassinated by his own retainers.
One night at dinner, the King's emissary gave the Pope

gossip so delicious that out of merriment, and about to vomit

from indulgence, he agreed
to free me. I owed King Francis

my art, my service. The same stipend he once paid

Leonardo, he now paid me; along with a house in Paris.
This house was, in truth, a castle . . .

I omitted, of course, quarrels with the King's

mistress, demon who taunted me for the slowness
of my work, out of her petty hatred of art itself;

omitted her insistence to the King that I

am insolent and by example teach
insolence to others. Omitted that I overheard the King

joke with her lieutenant: —

Kill him, if you can find me
his equal in art.

Before the school of Florence I had only been able,

young, to show myself as goldsmith
and jeweler; not yet as sculptor.

Duke Cosimo then announced that all the King of France

had given me, he would surpass: boasting,
he beckoned me to follow him past the public

common galleries, into the private apartments . . .

Dutiful abashed puppet, I followed; I knew
I would remain and make his statue.

              •

In the mirror of art, you who are familiar with the rituals of
decorum and bloodshed before which you are

silence and submission

while within stone
the mind writhes

contemplate, as if a refrain were wisdom, the glistening

intrication
of bronze and will and circumstance in the mirror of art.

·

Bandinelli for months insinuated in the Duke's ear
Perseus never would be finished:—

I lacked the art, he said, to move from the small

wax model the Duke rightly praised, to lifesize
bronze whose secrets tormented even Donatello.

So eighteen months after work began, Duke Cosimo grew

tired, and withdrew his subsidy. Lattanzo Gorini,
spider-handed and gnat-voiced, refusing to hand over

payment said, *Why do you not finish?*

Then Bandinelli hissed *Sodomite!* at
me—after my enumeration, to the court's

amusement, of the sins against art and sense

committed by his *Hercules and Cacus*, recital
designed to kill either him or his authority. . . .

The Duke, at the ugly word, frowned

and turned away. I replied that the sculptor of
Hercules and Cacus must be a madman to think that I

presumed to understand the art that Jove in heaven

used on Ganymede, art nobly practiced here on earth
by so many emperors and kings. My saucy speech

ended: *My poor wick does not dare to burn so high!*

Duke and court broke into laughter. Thus was
born my resolve to murder Bandinelli.

    •

I'd hurl the creature to hell. In despair at what must
follow—the Duke's rage, abandonment of my

never-to-be-born Perseus—I cast

myself away for lost: with a hundred crowns
and a swift horse, I resolved first to bid

farewell to my natural son, put to wet-nurse in Fiesole;

then to descend to San Domenico, where Bandinelli
returned each evening. *Then, after blood, France.*

Reaching Fiesole, I saw the boy

was in good health; his wet-nurse
was my old familiar, old gossip, now

married to one of my workmen. The boy

clung to me: wonderful in a two-year-old, in
grief he flailed his arms when at last

in the thick half-dusk

I began to disengage myself. Entering the square
of San Domenico on one side, I saw my prey

arriving on the other. Enraged that he still

drew breath, when I reached him
I saw he was unarmed. He rode a small sorry

mule. A wheezing donkey carried a ten-year-old

boy at his side. In my sudden presence, his face
went white. I nodded my head and rode past.

•

I had a vision of Bandinelli surrounded
by the heaped-up works of his hand.

Not one thing that he had made

did I want to have made.
From somewhere within his body

like a thread

he spun the piles surrounding him. Then he
tried to pull away, to release the thread; I saw

the thread was a leash.

He tried and tried to cut it.
At this, in my vision I said out-loud: —

My art is my revenge.

.

When I returned to Florence from Fiesole, after
three days news was brought to me that my little boy

was smothered by his wet-nurse

turning over on him as they both slept.
His panic, as I left; his arms raised, in panic.

.

*from the great unchosen narration you will soon
be released*

Benvenuto Cellini

*dirtied by blood and earth
but now*

you have again taught yourself to disappear

moving wax from arm
to thigh

you have again taught yourself to disappear

here where each soul is its
orbit spinning

sweetly around the center of itself

at the edge of its eye the great
design of virtue

here your Medusa and your Perseus are twins

his triumphant body still furious with purpose
but his face abstracted absorbed in

contemplation as she is

abstracted absorbed
though blood still spurts from her neck

defeated by a mirror

as in concentration you move wax
from thigh to arm

under your hand it grows

The idyll began when the Duke reached me a goldsmith's
hammer, with which I struck the goldsmith's

chisel he held; and so the little statues were

disengaged from earth and rust. Bronze
antiquities, newly found near Arezzo, they lacked

either head or hands or feet. Impatient for my

presence, the Duke insisted that I join him each evening
at his new pastime, playing artisan — leaving orders

for my free admittance to his rooms, day or night.

His four boys, when the Duke's eyes were turned,
hovered around me, teasing. One night

I begged them to hold their peace.

The boldest replied, *That we can't do!* I said
what one cannot do is required of no one.

So have your will! Faced with their sons'

delight in this new principle, the Duke and Duchess
smiling accused me of a taste for chaos. . . .

At last the four figures wrought for the four

facets of the pedestal beneath Perseus
were finished. I brought them one evening to the Duke,

arranging them on his worktable in a row: —

figures, postures from scenes that the eye cannot
entirely decipher, story haunting the eye with its

resonance, unseen ground that explains nothing. . . .

The Duke appeared, then immediately
retreated; reappearing, in his right hand

he held a pear slip. *This is for your garden, the garden of*

your house. I began, *Do you mean,* but he cut me off
saying, *Yes, Benvenuto: garden and house now are yours.*

Thus I received what earlier was only lent me.

I thanked him and his Duchess; then both
took seats before my figures.

For two hours talk was of their beauty, —

the Duchess insisted they were too exquisite
to be wasted down there

in the piazza; I must place them in her apartments.

No argument from intention or design
unconvinced her.

So I waited till the next day—entering the private

chambers at the hour the Duke and Duchess
each afternoon went riding, I carried the statues

down and soldered them with lead into their niches.

Returning, how angry the Duchess became! The Duke
abandoned his workshop. I went there no more.

·

The old inertia of earth that hates the new
(as from a rim I watched)

rose from the ground, legion:—

truceless ministers of the great unerasable
ZERO, eager to annihilate lineament and light,

waited, pent, against the horizon:—

some great force (*massive, stubborn, multiform as
earth, fury whose single name is LEGION,—*)

wanted my Perseus not to exist:—

and I must
defeat them.

Then my trembling assistants woke me.

They said all my work
was spoiled.

Perseus was spoiled. He lay buried in earth

wreathed in fragile earthenware veins from the furnace
above, veins through which he still

waited to be filled with burning metal.

The metal was curdled. As I slept, sick,
the bronze had been allowed to cake, to curdle.

Feverish, made sick by my exertions for

days, for months, I slept; while those charged
with evenly feeding the furnace that I had so well

prepared, LARKED—

I thought, *Unwitting ministers of the gorgon
Medusa herself.* The furnace choked with caking, curdling

metal that no art known to man could

uncurdle, must be utterly dismantled—all
who made it agreed this must destroy

the fragile, thirsty mould of Perseus beneath.

But Perseus was not more strong
than Medusa, but more clever:—if he ever

was to exist as idea, he must first exist as matter: —

all my old inborn
daring returned,

furious to reverse

the unjust triumphs of the world's mere
arrangements of power, that seemingly on earth

cannot be reversed. First, I surveyed my forces: —

seven guilty workmen, timid, sullen,
resentful; a groom; two maids; a cook.

I harassed these skeptical troops into battle: —

two hands were sent to fetch from the butcher
Capretta a load of young oak, —

in bronze furnaces the only woods you use

are slow-burning alder, willow, pine: now I needed
oak and its fierce heat. As the oak

was fed log by log into the fire, how the cake began

to stir, to glow and sparkle. Now
from the increased

combustion of the furnace, a conflagration

shot up from the roof: two windows
burst into flame: I saw the violent storm

filling the sky fan the flames.

All the while with pokers and iron rods
we stirred and stirred the channels—

the metal, bubbling, refused to flow.

I sent for all my pewter plates, dishes, porringers—
the cooks and maids brought some two hundred.

Piece by piece, I had them thrown

into the turgid mass. As I watched the metal for
movement, the cap of the furnace

exploded—bronze welling over on all sides.

I had the plugs pulled, the mouths of the mould
opened; in perfect liquefaction

the veins of Perseus filled. . . .

Days later, when the bronze had cooled, when the clay
sheath had been with great care removed, I found

what was dead brought to life again.

•

Now, my second
prison. It began soon after Perseus was unveiled

to acclaim—great acclaim. Perhaps I grew

too glorious. Perseus, whose birth consumed
nine years, found stuck to his pedestal

sonnets celebrating the master's hand that made him. . . .

On the day of unveiling, Duke Cosimo stationed himself
at a window just above the entrance to the palace;

there, half-hidden, he listened for hours to the crowd's

wonder. He sent his attendant Sforza to say
my reward

soon would astonish me.

Ten days passed. At last Sforza appeared and asked
what price I placed on my statue.

I was indeed astonished: *It is not my custom,*

I replied, *to set a price for my work, as if
he were a merchant and I a mere tradesman.*

Then, at risk of the Duke's severe displeasure, I was

warned I must set a price: infuriated, I said
ten thousand golden crowns.

Cities and great palaces are built with ten thousand

golden crowns, the Duke
two days later flung at me in anger.

Many men can build cities and palaces,

I replied, *but not one can make
a second Perseus.*

Bandinelli, consulted by the Duke, reluctantly

concluded that the statue was worth
sixteen thousand.

The Duke replied that for two farthings

Perseus could go to the scrap heap; that would
resolve our differences.

At last, the settlement was thirty-five hundred, one

hundred a month. Soon after, charges were brought
against me, for sodomy—

I escaped Florence as far as Scarperia, but there

the Duke's soldiers caught me and in chains
brought me back.

I confessed. If I had not, I could have been made

to serve as a slave in the Duke's galleys for life.
The Duke listened behind a screen as I was made

publicly to confess, in full court. . . . Punishment

was *four years* imprisonment. Without the Duke's
concurrence, of course, no charges could have been

lodged, no public humiliation arranged

to silence the insolent. *The first Cosimo, founder of Medici
power, all his life protected Donatello—whose*

affections and bliss were found in Ganymede.

After imprisonment one month, Cosimo
finally commuted my sentence to house arrest.

There his magnanimity allowed me to complete

my Christ of the whitest marble
set upon a cross of the blackest.

Now, my Christ sits still packed in a crate

in the Duke's new chapel; my bust of the Duke
is exiled to Elba, there to frighten in open air

slaves peering out from his passing galleys.

Now, after the Duchess and two of their sons
died of fever within two months, Cosimo

grows stranger: he murdered Sforza

by running him through with a spear: —
he does not own

his mind; or will.

When I ask release from his service, he says
that he cannot, that he soon

will have need of me for great projects; no

commissions come. Catherine de' Medici, regent of
the young French king, petitioned that I be allowed

to enter her service. He said I had no will now to work.

In prison I wrote my sonnet addressed
to Fortune: — *Fortune, you sow!*

You turned from me because Ganymede

also is my joy. . . . O God of Nature, author
of my nature,

where does your son Jesus forbid it?

When I was five, one night my father
woke me. He pulled me to the basement, making me

stare into the oak fire and see what he just had seen.

There a little lizard was sporting
at the core of the intensest flames.

My father boxed me on the ears, then kissed me —

saying that I must remember this night: —
My dear little boy, the lizard you see

is a salamander, a creature that lives

at the heart of fire. You and I are blessed: no other
soul now living has been allowed to see it.

•

I am too old to fight to leave Florence: —

here, young, this goldsmith and jeweler
began to imagine that

severity, that *chastity* of style

certain remnants of the ancient world
left my hand hungry to emulate: —

equilibrium of ferocious, contradictory

forces: equilibrium whose balance or poise is their
tension, and does not efface them, —

as if the surface of each thing

arranged within the frame, the surface of each
body the eye must circle

gives up to the eye its vibration, its nature.

Two or three times, perhaps, —*you
say where,* —I have achieved it.

                    •

See, in my great bronze bust of the great
Duke, embedded in the right epaulette like a trophy
an open-mouthed
face part lion part man part goat, with an iron
bar jammed in its lower jaw

rising resistlessly across its mouth.

See, in Vasari's clumsy portrait of me, as I float
above the right shoulder of the Duke, the same face."

                    •

*As if your hand fumbling to reach inside
reached inside*

*As if light falling on the surface
fell on what made the surface*

*As if there were no scarcity of sun
on the sun*

I covered my arm with orchid juice.

With my hatchet I split a mangrove stick
from a tree, and sharpened it.

I covered the killing stick with orchid juice.

We were camping at Marunga Island
looking for oysters. This woman I was about to kill

at last separated herself from the others

to hunt lilies. She walked into the swamp, then
got cold, and lay down on sandy ground.

After I hit her between the eyes with my hatchet

she kicked, but couldn't
raise up.

With my thumb over the end of the killing stick

I jabbed her Mount of Venus until her skin pushed
back up to her navel. Her large intestine

protruded as though it were red calico.

With my thumb over the end of the killing stick
each time she inhaled

I pushed my arm

in a little. When she exhaled, I stopped. Little by little
I got my hand

inside her. Finally I touched her heart.

Once you reach what is
inside it is outside. I pushed the killing stick

into her heart.

The spirit that belonged to that dead woman
went into my heart then.

I felt it go in.

I pulled my arm
out. I covered my arm with orchid juice.

Next I broke a nest of green ants

off a tree, and watched the live ants
bite her skin until her skin moved by itself

downward from her navel and covered her bones.

Then I took some dry mud and put my sweat
and her blood in the dry mud

and warmed it over a fire. Six or eight times

I put the blood and sweat and mud
inside her uterus until there was no trace of her

wound or what I had done.

I was careful none of her pubic hair was left
inside her vagina for her husband to feel.

Her large intestine stuck out several feet.

When I shook some green ants on it, a little
went in. I shook some more. All of it went in.

When I whirled the killing stick with her heart's blood

over her head, her head
moved. When I whirled it some more, she moved

more. The third time I whirled the killing stick

she gasped for breath. She blew some breath
out of her mouth, and was all right.

I said, *You go eat some lilies.* She

got up. I said, *You will live
two days. One day you will be happy. The next, sick.*

She ate some lilies. She walked around, then

came back and slept. When laughing and talking women
woke her she gathered her lilies and returned to camp.

The next day she walked around and played,

talked and made fun, gathering with others oysters
and lilies. She brought into camp what she

gathered. That night she lay down and died.

Even the gods cannot
end death. In this universe anybody can kill anybody

with a stick. What the gods gave me

is *their* gift, the power to bury within each
creature the hour it ceases.

Everyone knows I have powers but not such power.

If they knew I would be so famous
they would kill me.

I tell you because your tongue is stone.

If the gods ever give you words, one night in
sleep you will wake to find me above you.

     •

After sex & metaphysics, —
. . . what?

What you have made.

     •

Infinite the forms, finite
tonight as I find again in the mirror the familiar appeaseless

eater's face

Ignorant of cause or source or end
in silence he repeats

Eater, become food

All life exists at the expense of other life
Because you have eaten and eat as eat you must

Eater, become food

unlike the burning stars
burning merely to be

Then I ask him how to become food

In silence he repeats that others have
other fates, but that I must fashion out of the corruptible

body a new body good to eat a thousand years

Then I tell the eater's face that within me is no
sustenance, on my famished

plate centuries have been served me and still I am famished

He smirks, and in silence repeats that all life exists
at the expense of other life

You must fashion out of the corruptible
body a new body good to eat a thousand years

Because you have eaten and eat as eat you must
ignorant of cause or source or end

•

drugged to sleep by repetition of the diurnal
round, the monotonous sorrow of the finite,

within   I am awake

repairing in dirt the frayed immaculate thread
forced by being to watch the birth of suns

•

This is the end of the third hour of the night.

NOTES

I *Music Like Dirt*

K.218 is Mozart's Fourth Violin Concerto. The phrase *music like dirt* is a refrain in Desmond Dekker's song "Intensified." I have never met Mr. Dekker; he is not the "you" of "Music Like Dirt." Think of "Advice to the Players" as a manifesto written by someone who does not believe in manifestos. Think of "Injunction" as the injunction heard by an artist faced with the forever warring elements of the world that proceed from the forever unreconciled elements of our nature. "Lament For the Makers" is the title of a poem by the Scots writer William Dunbar (1460?–1520?).

I hoped to make a sequence in which the human need to make is seen as not only central but inescapable. I wanted not a tract, but a tapestry in which making is seen in the context of the other processes—sexuality, mortality—inseparable from it.

II

"Curse": The "you" addressed here brought down the World Trade Center towers; when I wrote the poem I didn't imagine that it could be read in any other way, though it has been. The poem springs from the ancient moral idea (the idea of Dante's *Divine Comedy*) that what is suffered for an act should correspond to the nature of the act. Shelley in his *Defense of Poetry* says that "the great secret of morals is love"—and by love he means not affection or erotic feeling, but sympathetic identification, identification with others. The "secret," hidden ground of how to act morally is entering the skin of another, imagination of what is experienced as the result of your act. Identification is here called down as punishment, the great secret of morals reduced to a curse.

"Hadrian's Deathbed": Hadrian, "Animula vagula blandula."

"Song": "It takes talent to live at night, and that was the one ability I never doubted I had" (Ava Gardner, *Ava: My Story*, 1990). "It's not raining inside tonight" (Johnny Standley, "It's In the Book," 1952).

"The Third Hour of the Night": In Part II, my largest debts are to John Addington Symonds's translation *The Life of Benvenuto Cellini, Written by Himself* (1887); and to Michael W. Cole's *Cellini and the Principles of Sculpture* (2002). Part III, section one, is based on W. Lloyd Warner's *A Black Civilization* (1958), pages 198–200; reprinted under the title "Black Magic: An Australian Sorcerer (Arnhem Land)" in Mircea Eliade's *From Primitives to Zen: A Thematic Sourcebook of the History of Religions* (1977; 443–45).

F.B.

AN INTERVIEW WITH FRANK BIDART

by Adam Travis, *Bookslut.com*

So far you've published "The First Hour of the Night," "The Second Hour of the Night," and "The Third Hour of the Night"—what is the inspiration for this project? That is, what made you want to do this? Where is it going? Does the project have a name?

The myth behind the series of poems is the Egyptian "Book of Gates," which is inscribed on the sarcophagus of Seti I. Each night during the twelve hours of the night the sun must pass through twelve territories of the underworld before it can rise again at dawn. Each hour is marked by a new gate, the threshold to a new territory.

Each poem in the series is an hour we must pass through before the sun can rise again. I don't know what will make moral and intellectual clarity and coherence rise again: I could never write twelve "hours." But were the sun to rise again, it would have to pass through something like these territories.

I've written only three "hours" over something like seventeen years. I'm sixty-six: I'll be lucky if I can write one more. I like the idea that I'm involved in a project that can't be completed: the project corresponds to how things are.

What is your favorite hour of the night? (I mean literally. Not which poem.)

It's easier to say which poem I like best! Of course, the way that I imagine each "territory" that the sun must pass through to rise again is different from the way someone else would imagine it. The "First Hour" is about the collapse of Western metaphysics, the attempt to make a single conceptual system that orders the crucial intellectual issues and dilemmas in our lives. At the end of the poem there is a dream that suggests the birth of something like phenomenology, the phenomenological ground out of which art springs, that survives the death of metaphysical certainty. The "Second Hour" is about Eros, how the "givenness" of Eros in our lives embodies the givenness of fate. The "Third Hour," which ends my new book, is about making, how "Making is the mirror in which we see ourselves." Making in the poem, and the book as a whole, proceeds from the twins within us, the impulse to create as well as not-to-create, to obliterate the world of manifestation, to destroy. (One of the many wars within us.)

I don't imagine the poems printed together as a series, one "hour" read after another hour. They are more like symphonies: you don't listen to Beethoven's symphonies consecutively, as you at least initially read the *Iliad* or even (perhaps) the *Duino Elegies*. But the fact that Beethoven's Fifth follows the Third and Fourth has meaning, as does the fact that the "Pastorale" follows the Fifth.

From the readers' perspective, the project has the makings of what one could call your Great Work. Do you have that kind of ambition? The subjects and their presentation seem almost designed to inspire awe. Is that what you're after?
I'm after something that will make some sense out of the chaos in the world and within us. The result should be something that is, well, "beautiful": but beauty isn't merely the pretty, or harmony, or equilibrium. Rilke says beauty is the beginning of terror: I feel this reading *King Lear*, or watching *Red Desert*.

I like to memorize long poems (to show off). Would you think me a fool for memorizing an hour of the night?
If the pulse of the poem is right, if the essential movement of the poem captures the essential pulse of the processes that the poem *sees*, one should be able to memorize it. At one time I could say the whole of "Second Hour" to myself, hearing the poem as I lay in bed.

When "The Third Hour of the Night" (about Benvenuto Cellini) appeared in the October 2004 issue of Poetry, *readers seemed to react only in one of two ways: awe or outrage. One common complaint was that the poem took up the entire issue (besides the "Comment" section). The logic here being that the poem is, supposedly, not good enough to have its own issue. Another complaint was that the poem read too much like prose, or was too obscure or esoteric or whatever. The final complaint was something like revulsion. The poem contains disturbing scenes of murder and some sort of ritual/sexual violence. These complaints beg a couple of questions: "How much of a long poem can actually consist of 'poetry'?" And: "These poems really are very violent. Why?"*
If a poem is any good, I don't think of some parts as "poetry" and other parts as "not poetry." Each line has to be written with a feeling for its place in the shape, the pulse of the whole: if it does that, it is authentically part of the *whatness* of the thing. It then has its own eloquence.

I think the question of violence is only a question because people think of poetry as lyric poetry. In lyric there is often a great deal of psychic violence, but usually little (say) murder. (Even in Browning's lyrics.) A heart gets eaten in the first sonnet of Dante's "Vita Nuova," but that is the exception.

But violence is at the heart of Dante's long poem, as it is incessant in Shakespeare. Or Sophocles. It is offstage, but barely, in Racine. It is not offstage in Virgil.

Can you explain what's going on in the last, very violent scene of "The Third Hour of the Night"?

With my thumb over the end of the killing stick

I jabbed her Mount of Venus until her skin pushed
back up to her navel. Her large intestine

protruded as though it were red calico.

With my thumb over the end of the killing stick
each time she inhaled

I pushed my arm

in a little. When she exhaled, I stopped. Little by little
I got my hand

inside her. Finally I touched her heart.

Once you reach what is
inside it is outside.

This is from a four-page monologue that is based on the words of an Australian sorcerer, found in a book by Mircea Eliade on the history of religions. With an appalling neutrality and evenness of tone the speaker is describing a kind of rape. At first you think he is also describing a killing, that he has murdered the woman. (The anthropologist quoted in Eliade says that in his village he is known as a murderer.) Then he says that after touching her heart and covering up the signs of what he has done, she begins to breathe again. He tells her that she will live two days, that after two days she will die. She gets up, and two days later dies.

The passage is clearly about the will to power, to possess the woman by entering her, the fantasy of controlling her by determining when she will die. I have no idea what "actually" happened. Did a woman from his village simply die and the sorcerer imagine that he had control over this process? Or did he rape, and later murder her? On the literal level, his report cannot be believed: he could not have done what he reports doing. He has tried to master whatever happened by constructing a narrative that could not literally be true.

What is true is the will to power. He fantasizes that he has the same power that the third Fate, earlier in the poem, has: the power to determine when someone dies. He admits he cannot keep the woman alive forever: all he can do is determine when the thread of life is slit. In the poem he says this power is the same power the gods have: "Even the gods cannot / end death." After his psychic rape of the woman, which involves the attempt to touch and therefore know her "heart," all he can do is turn her into a kind of puppet: he tells her she will live two days, and she then enacts this. This is a terrible parody of what Cellini does earlier in the poem, when he saves the almost-ruined statue of Perseus and "what was dead [was] brought to life again." It is the terrible, negative version of the injunction the central consciousness of the whole poem hears *after* the monologue by the sorcerer: he "must fashion out of the corruptible / body a new body good to eat a thousand years." (Which is to say, echoing "Howl," that one must try to make what in despair one feels is impossible to make, a good poem.)

The whole book is about making, how the desire to make is built into us, its necessities and pleasures and contradictions. The impulse to make is itself neither good nor bad. It is a species of the will to power, which is inseparable from survival and creation. It is inseparable from the impulse to destroy. The most ferocious enactment of the will to power always must confront metaphysical and epistemological limits: in the poem (not in Eliade): "Once you reach what is / inside it is outside." Human beings constantly strive to reach the heart of something: when they reach it they find it is only another surface. Art strives to be that center that has reached the light, and remains the center: in Ashbery's brilliant phrase, the "visible core."

JUNE 2005